Masterbuilt Smoker Cookbook

The Ultimate

Masterbuilt Electric Smoker Cookbook

Simple and Delicious Masterbuilt Electric Smoker Recipes for Your Whole Family

Billy Yothers

Copyright © Billy Yothers 2018

All rights reserved.

MASTERBUILT SMOKER COOKBOOK

TABLE OF CONTENTS

1	Poultry Recipes Using Masterbuilt Smoker	4
2	Seafood Recipes Using Masterbuilt Smoker	17
3	Pork Recipes Using Masterbuilt Smoker	33
4	Beef Recipes Using Masterbuilt Smoker	48
5	Conclusion	62

MASTERBUILT SMOKER COOKBOOK

COPYRIGHT 2018 BY BILLY YOTHERS - ALL RIGHTS RESERVED

This document is geared towards providing exact and reliable information in regard to the topic and issue covered. The publication is sold on the idea that the publisher is not required to render an accounting, officially permitted, or otherwise, qualified services. If advice is necessary, legal or professional, a practiced individual in the profession should be ordered.

From a Declaration of Principles which was accepted and approved equally by a Committee of the American Bar Association and a Committee of Publishers and Associations.

In no way is it legal to reproduce, duplicate, or transmit any part of this document by either electronic means or in printed format. Recording of this publication is strictly prohibited and any storage of this document is not allowed unless with written permission from the publisher. All rights reserved.

The information provided herein is stated to be truthful and consistent, in that any liability, in terms of inattention or otherwise, by any usage or abuse of any policies, processes, or directions contained within is the solitary and utter responsibility of the recipient reader. Under no circumstances will any legal responsibility or blame be held against the publisher for any reparation, damages, or monetary loss due to the information herein, either directly or indirectly.

Respective authors own all copyrights not held by the publisher. The information herein is offered for informational purposes solely and is universal as so. The presentation of the information is without a contract or any type of guarantee assurance.

The trademarks that are used are without any consent, and the publication of the trademark is without permission or backing by the trademark owner. All trademarks and brands within this book are for clarifying purposes only and are the owned by the owners themselves, not affiliated with this document.

POULTRY RECIPES USING MASTERBUILT SMOKER

SMOKED THANKSGIVING TURKEY

SERVING SIZE: 1
SERVINGS PER RECIPE: 12
CALORIES: 384
COOKING TIME: 7 HOURS

INGREDIENTS:

- Turkey—12–14 pounds
- Extra-virgin olive oil—3 tablespoons
- Unsalted butter—3 tablespoons
- Fresh garlic—2 cloves, minced
- Dried thyme—2 tablespoons
- Powdered sage—1 tablespoon
- Dried oregano—2 teaspoons
- Paprika—2 teaspoons
- Sea salt—2 teaspoons
- Cracked black pepper—1 ½ teaspoons
- Dried rosemary—1 teaspoon
- Apple—1, cut into quarters
- Lemon or orange—1, cut into quarters
- Medium onion—1, cut into half
- Apple cider—1/2 cup
- Water—½ cup
- Apple or pecan woodchips

MASTERBUILT SMOKER COOKBOOK

NUTRITION INFORMATION:

Carbohydrate—26.4g

Protein—46.2g

Fat—10.2 g

Sodium—4,080 mg

Cholesterol—186 mg

INSTRUCTIONS:

1. Take a drip pan and bowl of water covered with aluminum foil. Preheat the smoker up to 225°F.

2. Take a small bowl for whipping the olive oil and butter together. Add the garlic, spices, and herbs to it.

3. Use $^1/_3{}^{rd}$ of the mixture to rub the inside of the turkey. Use the fruits and onion to stuff inside the turkey. Use the remaining herb, spice, and butter mixture to rub the outside of the bird.

4. Use water and apple cider to fill the water pan halfway. Place the drip pan above the water pan. Use woodchips to fill the side tray.

5. Put the turkey in the middle rack of the electric smoker. You would want to get an inside temperature of ~~165~~ 185°F. Use a digital thermometer to check the inside temperature of the bird. Set the smoker for 6 ½ hours, which is roughly the required time.

6. Keep a check on the woodchips in case the smoke reduces. Add in more woodchips in that case. Also, keep an eye on the water pan. Add in more liquid if required.

7. Remove the turkey carefully from the smoker when cooked. Place it on a cutting board and let it rest for 20 minutes before carving. Your dish is ready to be served.

SMOKED CHICKEN WRAP

SERVING SIZE: 4
SERVINGS PER RECIPE: 2
CALORIES: 533
COOKING TIME: 3 HOURS

INGREDIENTS:

　Chicken breasts—2 (small)

　Romaine hearts

　Tomato—1, diced

　Parmesan cheese—shavings

　Caesar salad dressing

　Salt—1 teaspoon

　Pepper—1 teaspoon

　Garlic powder—½ teaspoon

　Large tortillas—4

NUTRITION INFORMATION:

　Carbohydrate—52.2g

　Protein—31.4g

　Fat—23.2 g

　Sodium—1,523 mg

　Cholesterol—86 mg

INSTRUCTIONS:

1. Bring up the temperature of the electric smoker to 225°F by preheating.

2. Take a large bowl. Place the chicken breasts in it. Season the breasts with salt, pepper, and garlic powder.

3. Place the chicken in the electric smoker and smoke it for about an hour and a half or let it cook until the chicken breasts reach an internal temperature of 165°F.

4. Remove the chicken when done. Let it rest for 10 minutes. Then, cut it up into slices.

5. Take a large mixing bowl and toss in the romaine hearts, Caesar dressing, and the Parmesan cheese shavings. Mix it well.

6. Warm up the tortillas on a flat pan on the stove.

7. Once the tortillas are well toasted, place them on a tray.

8. Put a layer of the salad, tomatoes, chicken slices, and a spoonful on Caesar dressing onto the tortillas.

9. Fold them up in rolls.

10. Your dish is ready to be served.

SMOKED CHICKEN SALAD WITH MANGO AND AVOCADO

SERVING SIZE: 1
SERVINGS PER RECIPE: 4
CALORIES: 372
COOKING TIME: 1 HOUR AND 30 MINUTES

INGREDIENTS:

FOR SMOKING THE CHICKEN:

- Chicken breasts—4, 4 ounces, boneless and skinless
- Tom Douglas chicken rub—1 tablespoon (you can use any rub of your choice)

FOR THE SALAD:

- Sweet chili sauce—2 tablespoons
- Lemon or lime juice—3 tablespoons
- Extra-virgin olive oil—2 tablespoons
- Mango—1, ripe, sliced
- Telegraph cucumber—½, halved lengthwise and sliced
- Cherry tomatoes—1, cut into half
- Red onion—1/2, thinly sliced
- Avocado—1, firm ripe, sliced
- Basil leaves—large, handful
- Mesclun leaves—4, handfuls

NUTRITION INFORMATION:

Carbohydrate—27g

Protein—24g

Fat—18 g

Sodium—654mg

Cholesterol—94 mg

INSTRUCTIONS:

1. Preheat the electric smoker and prepare it with woodchips.

2. Take the chicken breasts and place them on a large tray. Rub the breasts well with the dry rub.

3. Carefully place the chicken breasts inside the electric smoker at about 300°F for nearly 1 hour.

4. Allow the chicken to cook for an hour. Make sure the internal temperature of the chicken is at least 165°F. When done, set it aside and allow it to rest for 5 minutes.

5. Slice up the breast into bite-size pieces for the salad.

6. Take a medium-size bowl. Whisk in the sweet chili sauce, extra-virgin olive oil, and the lemon juice for making the dressing for the salad. Season the dressing with salt and pepper.

7. Take a large salad bowl. Add in the dressing with the cut-up mango, red onion, cucumber, tomatoes, avocado, basil, mesclun, and the sliced up smoked chicken. Add in a dash of lemon if wanted.

8. Your dish is ready to be served.

BACON WRAPPED SMOKED CHICKEN

SERVING SIZE: 1

SERVINGS PER RECIPE: 6

CALORIES: 479

COOKING TIME: 3 HOURS AND 30 MINUTES

INGREDIENTS:

- Chicken breasts—6
- Bacon—12 strips
- BBQ dry rub—6 tablespoons
- Cherry wood—3 chunks

BRINE:

- Water—4 cups
- Kosher salt—1/4 cup
- Brown sugar—1/4 cup
- Peppercorns—1/2 teaspoon
- Garlic—4 cloves, crushed

NUTRITION INFORMATION:

- Carbohydrate—1.7g
- Protein—30g
- Fat—22.7 g
- Sodium—270mg
- Cholesterol—40mg

INSTRUCTIONS:

1. Take a saucepan and place it on a medium flame. Add in all the brine ingredients into the pan and mix well. Let it start bubbling and dissolve all the sugar and salt. Set it aside to cool.

2. Take a gallon bag and pour in all the brine into it. Add in the chicken breasts into the bag and seal it. Allow the brine to mix well with the chicken. Let it sit in the refrigerator for 2 hours.

3. Remove chicken soaked in brine from the refrigerator. Pick up the chicken breasts from the brine liquid and wash it under running water to remove excess salt or sugar.

4. Apply the BBQ dry rub on the chicken breasts.

5. Wrap two pieces of bacon on each chicken breast. Wrap it tightly around the chicken from top to bottom and secure it with toothpicks.

6. The electric smoker needs to be preheated to 275°F. Add 3 chunks of cherry wood in the electric smoker on top of the charcoal while cooking.

7. Allow the chicken to smoke until the chicken breast reaches the temperature of 165°F or cook for at least 60–90 minutes.

8. Flip the chicken once when cooked halfway.

9. Remove the chicken from the smoker when done. Allow it to rest for 15 minutes and your dish is ready to be served.

SMOKED CHICKEN AND GUACAMOLE SANDWICH

SERVING SIZE: 1
SERVINGS PER RECIPE: 2
CALORIES: 390
COOKING TIME: 1 HOUR

INGREDIENTS:

  Chicken breasts—2

  Avocados—ripe, 2

  Tomato—1, diced

  Onion—1, diced

  Lime—1

  Salt—1 teaspoon

  Garlic powder—1 teaspoon

  Cajun—1 teaspoon

  Multigrain bread—4 slices

NUTRITION INFORMATION:

  Carbohydrate—32g

  Protein—43g

  Fat—27 g

  Sodium—850 mg

  Cholesterol—170 mg

INSTRUCTIONS:

1. Prepare the electric smoker by preheating it to a temperature of 225°F.

2. Apply the Cajun seasoning to the chicken breasts generously.

3. Put the chicken inside the smoker and allow it to smoke the chicken for about an hour and a half. Make sure you smoke until the chicken breasts reach an internal temperature of 165°F.

4. Once done, set the chicken aside and allow it to rest for 10 minutes. Cut it up into thin slices.

5. Cut the avocado into halves. Remove the seeds and scoop out the flesh into a medium-size bowl.

6. Squeeze in half a lemon into the avocado. Mix it well with the help of a spoon to remove all lumps and bring it to a smooth paste.

7. Add in the chopped tomatoes and onion to avocado mixture and stir it well.

8. Pour in the remaining lime juice over the avocado mixture along with a pinch of salt and pepper.

9. Take a slice of the multigrain bread and apply a generous helping of the guacamole. If you wish, you can grill the bread too before applying the spread.

10. Lay the chicken slices on the bread one after the other. Top it off with another slice of bread.

11. Your dish is ready to be served.

SMOKED TURKEY WINGS WITH SAGE LEMON HONEY BUTTER DIP

SERVING SIZE: 1
SERVINGS PER RECIPE: 2
CALORIES: 180
COOKING TIME: 27 HOURS

INGREDIENTS:

BRINE:

- Onion—½, medium, peeled and quartered
- Fennel stems and fronds—3, rough chopped
- Fresh thyme—4–6 sprigs
- Bay leaves—2
- Peppercorns—6
- Kosher salt—½ cup
- Golden brown sugar—½ cup
- Water—8–9 cups

TURKEY:

- Turkey wings—2–4

DIP:

- Butter—½ cup
- Lemon juice—1 lemon (small)
- Honey—1/4 cup
- Sage—1 tablespoon, chopped

NUTRITION INFORMATION:

Carbohydrate—0g

Protein—26 g

Fat—8 g

Sodium—1,460 mg

Cholesterol—110mg

INSTRUCTIONS:
BRINE:

1. Take a medium-size cooking pot. Put it on medium flame on the stove. Add in the water and along with it all the other brine ingredients. Allow it to come to a boil. Mix it well to dissolve the sugar and salt.

2. Reduce the heat and let it simmer for a good 30 minutes.

3. Set it aside and let it cool down at room temperature.

4. Take a medium-size storage pan and lay the turkey wings in it. Pour in the brine over turkey wings.

5. Brine the turkey wings overnight or for 24 hours straight.

    Smoked turkey wings:

6. Pick out the turkey wings from the brine. Set it aside and let it dry completely. Remove all bits of herbs or spices stuck to the turkey wings.

7. Use any woodchips of your preference for the smoke. Usually, hickory wood is recommended for turkey.

8. Preheat the electric smoker and prep it up with the woodchips.

9. Place the turkey wings skin-side up in the electric smoker.

10. Allow the wings to smoke at 200°F until the wings reach the internal temperature of 15o°F.

11. Cut at joints of the wing pieces and slice them up.

DIP:

12. Take a medium-size saucepan and place it on low heat.

13. Add the butter to the pan and let it melt completely.

14. Add in the sage to the pan and give it a good mix.

15. Add in the honey and bring the mixture to a boil.

16. When it starts to bubble, turn off the heat. Add in the lemon juice along with a pinch of salt.

17. Place the hot and fresh turkey wings on a serving plate with a spoonful of the dip.

18. Your dish is ready to be served.

SEAFOOD RECIPES USING MASTERBUILT SMOKER

LEMON PEPPER SMOKED TUNA

SERVING SIZE: 1

SERVINGS PER RECIPE: 7

CALORIES: 235

COOKING TIME: 1 HOUR

INGREDIENTS:

- Tuna steaks—6 ounces, 1-inch thick
- Kosher salt—3 tablespoons
- Brown sugar—3 tablespoons
- Extra-virgin olive oil—¼ cup
- Lemon pepper seasoning
- Ground garlic—1 teaspoon
- Fresh lemon—12 thin slices
- Water
- Peach wood chips

NUTRITION INFORMATION:

- Carbohydrate—34 g
- Protein—32 g
- Fat—28 g
- Sodium—2,376 mg
- Cholesterol—240 mg

INSTRUCTIONS:

1. Place the tuna steaks on a plate. Sprinkle salt and sugar on all sides. Put the seasoned steaks inside a sealed packet. Let it refrigerate for about 4 hours.

2. Pour water at the bottom of the pan in the smoker. Put woodchips in the tray.

3. Preheat the electric smoker to a temperature of 190°F.

4. Put the tuna steaks on a plate and take off the dry brine from it. Season both sides of the tuna steaks with extra-virgin olive oil, garlic powder, and lemon pepper seasoning.

5. Now place the tuna steaks on the smoker rack and add two lemon slices on top of them. Put the rack inside the electric smoker and allow it to smoke for about an hour.

6. After an hour, check whether the steaks have attained an internal temperature of 145°F. Let it smoke for about 60 minutes in total, approximately.

7. Put the smoked tuna steaks on the cutting board and let it rest for some time.

8. Season it with fresh lime wedges or avocado slices.

9. Your dish is ready to be served.

SMOKED TROUT

SERVING SIZE: 1
SERVINGS PER RECIPE: 4
CALORIES: 382
COOKING TIME: 3 HOURS

INGREDIENTS:

Trout fillets—4

White cooking wine—1 cup

Soy sauce—¼ cup

Lemon juice—¼ cup

NUTRITION INFORMATION:

Carbohydrate—24g

Protein—63 g

Fat—16 g

Sodium—2,481 mg

Cholesterol—370 mg

INSTRUCTIONS:

1. Take a small bowl and add all the ingredients in it except the trout fillets. Mix it together.

2. Place the trout fillets on a plate and pour the marinade mix all over it. Make sure the trout fillets are covered in the marinade from all sides. Put it inside the refrigerator for about 6 hours or overnight.

3. Put the marinated trout fillets on the smoking tray and allow it to rest with exposure to dry air for about 30 minutes.

4. Preheat the Masterbuilt ElectricSmoker to 150°F.

5. Put the dried trout tray inside the smoker and allow it to smoke for about 45 minutes.

6. If you wish to increase the smoking temperature, adjust the temperature to 225°F.

7. Take out the smoked trout fillets from the smoker.

8. Your dish is ready to be served.

SMOKED FISH BRINE

SERVING SIZE: 1
SERVINGS PER RECIPE: 8
CALORIES: 208
COOKING TIME: 2 HOURS

INGREDIENTS:

- Fish fillets—8
- Water—2 quarts
- Brown sugar—1 cup
- Apple juice—1 cup
- Kosher salt—½ cup
- Soy sauce—1 cup
- Fresh ground black pepper—¾ teaspoon
- Onion salt—¼ teaspoon
- Garlic powder—¼ teaspoon
- Seasoning salt—1 teaspoon
- Hot sauce—4 dashes

NUTRITION INFORMATION:

Carbohydrate—23g

Protein—56 g

Fat—17 g

Sodium—237 mg

Cholesterol—39 mg

INSTRUCTIONS:

1. Take a large bowl and add all the ingredients in it. Stir till the salt dissolves in it.

2. Let your fish brine for about 6 hours. Take out the fish from the brine and put it on the smoking rack.

3. Set the temperature of electric smoker to 200°F. Let it smoke for about 2 hours until the internal temperature reaches 160°F.

4. Your dish is ready to be served.

SMOKED MUSSELS IN WHITE WINE SAUCE

SERVING SIZE: 1
SERVINGS PER RECIPE: 8
CALORIES: 391
COOKING TIME: 45 MINUTES

INGREDIENTS:

- Fresh mussels—1 kg, scrubbed, inspected
- Butter—4 tablespoons, unsalted
- Olive oil—1 tablespoon
- Garlic—1 clove, minced
- Shallots—2 tablespoons, minced
- Italian parsley—2 tablespoons, chopped
- Dry white wine—½
- Rosemary—1 twig
- Thyme—1 twig
- Pecan woodchips

NUTRITION INFORMATION:

- Carbohydrate—13 g
- Protein—20 g
- Fat—8 g
- Sodium—434 mg
- Cholesterol—320 mg

INSTRUCTIONS:

1. To prepare the mussels, rinse it under cold water and clean all the sand or barnacles.

2. With the help of a knife, give a tap on the shell of the open mussels. The ones that fail to close should be discarded. Discard the fibrous hairs and anything that floats on the top.

3. Fill a pot with the filtered liquid and put the mussels in it. Let it soak for about 20 minutes.

4. Set the electric smoker ready at a temperature of 145°F.

5. Take an aluminum foil and put the mussels in it. Put this inside the smoker. Add pecan woodchips inside the smoker to smoke it well.

6. Allow the mussels to smoke for about half an hour. Do not overcook them. Let it cook until the shells open up.

7. To make the sauce, take a saucepan and add butter and olive oil in it. Let it melt. Add garlic and shallots in it and allow it to cook for some more time.

8. To increase the heat, add white wine in it and let it cook for about 2 minutes until it starts reducing.

9. Decrease the heat and add thyme and rosemary in it.

10. Put the mussels in a serving bowl and drizzle the white wine sauce all over it.

11. Season it with parsley.

12. Your dish is ready to be served.

SMOKY CAJUN SHRIMP

SERVING SIZE: 1
SERVINGS PER RECIPE: 4
CALORIES: 250
COOKING TIME: 10 MINUTES

INGREDIENTS:

Extra-virgin olive oil—4 tablespoons

Lemon—1, juiced

Garlic cloves—2, finely minced

Cajun shake—1 tablespoon

Salt—1 teaspoon

Shrimp—2 pounds, raw, peeled and deveined

NUTRITION INFORMATION:

Carbohydrate—33 g

Protein—29 g

Fat—6 g

Sodium—850 mg

Cholesterol—150 mg

INSTRUCTIONS:
1. Take a zip lock bag and put all the ingredients in it. Shake it and gently toss the shrimps well.

2. Cover the shrimps and let it marinade for 3 hours or more.

3. Preheat the Masterbuilt ElectricSmoker at high heat setting for about 5 minutes. Once it is heated enough, place the shrimps in the rack by threading them onto skewers.

4. Allow the shrimps to cook on both sides for about 4 minutes each. Make sure the shrimps turn smoky enough.

5. Your dish is ready to be served.

SMOKED GARLICKY SHRIMP

SERVING SIZE: 1
SERVINGS PER RECIPE: 3
CALORIES: 186
COOKING TIME: 1 HOUR

INGREDIENTS:

Apple cider—1 cup

Ketchup—1 cup

Apple cider vinegar—½ cup

Whole grain mustard—2 tablespoons

Brown sugar—2 tablespoons

Worcestershire sauce—2 teaspoons

Smoked paprika—1 teaspoon

Dry mustard—½ teaspoon

Shrimp—2 pounds, medium, tail on, peeled and deveined

Olive oil—¼ cup

Parsley leaves—¼ cup, roughly chopped

Dry sherry—¼ cup

Lemon zest—2 teaspoons

Red pepper flakes—¼ teaspoon, crushed

Garlic cloves—4, minced

NUTRITION INFORMATION:

Carbohydrate—7 g

Protein—28 g

Fat—3 g

Sodium—814 mg

Cholesterol—173 mg

INSTRUCTIONS:

1. In a saucepan, add apple cider and let it reduce over medium-high heat for about 10 minutes. Now add the apple cider vinegar, ketchup, mustard, sugar, Worcestershire sauce, paprika, and dry mustard in it. Allow it to simmer and cook for about 30 minutes. The barbeque sauce should gain a thick consistency.

2. In a ziplock bag, add the shrimps, garlic, shallots, oil, sherry, parsley, lemon zest, and red pepper flakes in it. Now shake the ziplock bag well till the shrimps are well coated in it.

3. Put the ziplock bag inside the refrigerator and allow it to marinade for about an hour or so.

4. Set the smoker ready at medium-high heat. Place the marinated shrimps on the smoker rack and let it smoke for about 12 minutes. Cook until the shrimps are thoroughly cooked through.

5. Remove the shrimps from the smoker. Plate it on a serving dish. Serve it along with the prepared barbeque sauce.

6. Sprinkle salt on the shrimps as desired. Your dish is ready to be served.

SOUTHWEST SMOKED WHITEFISH

SERVING SIZE: 1
SERVINGS PER RECIPE: 5
CALORIES: 142
COOKING TIME: 2 HOURS

INGREDIENTS:

- Whitefish fillets—2 pounds, raw
- Paprika—1 tablespoon
- Garlic powder—1 tablespoon
- Onion powder—1 tablespoon
- Cumin—½ teaspoon
- Sea salt—to taste
- Pepper—to taste
- Olive oil—1 tablespoon
- Fresh lemon—juiced
- Fresh cilantro—chopped

NUTRITION INFORMATION:

- Carbohydrate—0 g
- Protein—30 g
- Fat—2 g
- Sodium—0 mg
- Cholesterol—13 mg

INSTRUCTIONS:

1. Set up the Masterbuilt ElectricSmoker at a temperature of 200°F on a low heat setting.

2. To create smoke, add smoked woodchips.

3. Brush the fish fillets with the olive oil.

4. In a bowl, add paprika, cumin, onion powder, garlic powder, salt, and pepper in it and mix it well. Rub this prepared seasoning all over the pork from all sides.

5. Spray some more olive oil on the fillets.

6. Place the seasoned fillets on the smoker rack and put it inside the electric smoker at a low temperature for about 2 hours.

7. Garnish it with fresh lemon juice and chopped cilantro.

8. Your dish is ready to be served.

SMOKY LOBSTER TAILS

SERVING SIZE: 1

SERVINGS PER RECIPE: 4

CALORIES: 160

COOKING TIME: 20 MINUTES

INGREDIENTS:

- Lobster tails—6
- Butter—¼ cup
- Garlic cloves—4

NUTRITION INFORMATION:

- Carbohydrate—0 g
- Protein—20 g
- Fat—1 g
- Sodium—490 mg
- Cholesterol—0 mg

INSTRUCTIONS:

1. First of all, preheat the Masterbuilt Electric Smoker to a temperature of 400°F.

2. With the help of kitchen scissors, open the lobster tails gently.

3. Take out the lobster meat gently from the shells but keep it inside the shells. Place it on a plate.

4. In a pan, add some butter and let it melt. Put some garlic cloves in it. Let it heat over medium-low heat.

5. Pour the garlic butter mixture all over the lobster tail meat. Let the smoker smoke the lobster meat until it reaches an internal temperature of 130°F.

6. Take out the smoked lobster meat from the smoker and set it aside. Pull out the lobster meat from the shells entirely with the help of a fork.

7. Pour some more garlic butter over it, if required.

8. Your dish is ready to be served.

PORK RECIPES USING MASTERBUILT SMOKER

COUNTRY-STYLE RIBS

SERVING SIZE: 1

SERVINGS PER RECIPE: 6

CALORIES: 251

COOKING TIME: 3 HOURS

INGREDIENTS:

- Country-style ribs—4 pounds
- Pork rub—to taste
- Apple juice—2 cups
- Butter—½ stick, melted
- BBQ sauce—18 ounces

NUTRITION INFORMATION:

- Carbohydrate—35 g
- Protein—76 g
- Fat—25 g
- Sodium—273 mg
- Cholesterol—20 mg

INSTRUCTIONS:

1. Season the country-style ribs from all sides.

2. Set the Masterbuilt Electric Smoker ready at a temperature of 275°F. Use fruitwoodchips.

3. Allow it to cook it for 1 hour and 15 minutes or until the ribs attain a temperature of 160°F.

4. Take a foil pan and mix melted butter, apple juice, and 16 ounces of BBQ sauce in it.

5. Put the ribs back in the pan and cover it up with foil.

6. Put it back in the Masterbuilt Electric Smoker until it reaches an internal temperature of 195°F. Allow it to cook it for another 1 hour and 15 minutes.

7. Take out the ribs from the liquid and place them on the racks. Glaze the ribs with the additional BBQ sauce and let it cook for about 10 minutes.

8. Now take out the ribs from the electric smoker and allow it to rest it for about 10 minutes.

9. Your dish is ready to be served.

SMOKED PORK AND BEANS

SERVING SIZE: 1
SERVINGS PER RECIPE: 5
CALORIES: 159
COOKING TIME: 3 HOURS AND 15 MINUTES

INGREDIENTS:

- Pork and beans—1 can, 16 ounces
- Shredded pork—1 cup
- Onion—$^1/_2$, minced
- Maple syrup—¼ cup
- Brown sugar—¼ cup
- Ketchup—½ cup
- Dijon ketchup—1 tablespoon
- Bacon strips—4, cooked, chopped

NUTRITION INFORMATION:

- Carbohydrate—18 g
- Protein—11 g
- Fat—2 g
- Sodium—176 mg
- Cholesterol—18 mg

INSTRUCTIONS:

1. First of all, set the smoker ready at a temperature of about 225°F.

2. In an aluminum pan, add both pork and beans into it.

3. Gradually, add the onions, shredded pork, maple syrup, brown sugar, mustard, ketchup, and bacon in it.

4. Let the electric smoker cook the pork for about 3 hours.

5. Take it out of the smoker and do cover it with a foil.

6. Let it cool down for about 10 minutes.

7. Your dish is ready to be served.

SMOKED CHEESY PORK BALLS

SERVING SIZE: 1
SERVINGS PER RECIPE: 8
CALORIES: 315
COOKING TIME: 1 HOUR

INGREDIENTS:

- Pork sausage—1 pound
- Ground pork—1 pound
- Jalapeno peppers—½ cup, finely diced
- Kosher salt—½ teaspoon
- Grilling rub for pork—2 teaspoons
- Plain breadcrumbs—¼ cup
- Egg—1
- Milk—¼ cup
- Jalapeno pepper jack cheese—1 kg, 8 ounces, cut into 18 cubes

NUTRITION INFORMATION:

- Carbohydrate—3 g
- Protein—17 g
- Fat—26 g
- Sodium—733 mg
- Cholesterol—71 mg

INSTRUCTIONS:

1. Set up the smoker at a temperature of 235°F.

2. In a bowl, add all the ingredients except the cheese.

3. Now divide the entire mixture into small portions, near about 16 balls.

4. In each portion, add a cube of cheese in it and again put the meat on the other side and roll it well into ball-shaped sizes. Now dust the pork balls with the pork rub.

5. Put the prepared pork balls inside the smoker and let it smoke for about an hour or so. Make sure the internal temperature reaches 160°F.

6. Take out the smoked balls from the electric smoker.

7. Your dish is ready to be served.

SPICED SMOKED PORK LOIN

SERVING SIZE: 1

SERVINGS PER RECIPE: 8

CALORIES: 301

COOKING TIME: 3 HOURS

INGREDIENTS:

Pork loin—6 pounds, whole

Chinese five-spice powder—1 tablespoon

Sea salt—2 tablespoons

Black pepper—1 teaspoon, cracked

Garlic powder—½ teaspoon

Nutmeg—¼ teaspoon

Grape-seed or safflower oil—2 tablespoons

Unsweetened apple juice

Water

NUTRITION INFORMATION:

Carbohydrate—47 g

Protein—62 g

Fat—22 g

Sodium—3,583 mg

Cholesterol—240 mg

INSTRUCTIONS:

1. First of all, make sure the pork loin is well washed and pat dry it with the help of a dry towel.

2. Trim off any excess fat from the pork loin and place it on a sheet pan.

3. Take a small bowl and add all the spices in it. Season the loin well with the mixture. Rub it from all sides.

4. Let it rest in the room temperature for about 60 minutes.

5. Preheat the Masterbuilt Electric Smoker to a temperature of 225°F.

6. At the base of the smoker, add 50% of the water and the apple juice in it. Put some woodchips at the side of the tray.

7. Now place the pork loin on the rack inside the smoker with its fat side facing up. Set the timer to 3 hours. Cook until the loin reaches an internal temperature of 155°F. Keep checking the meat at an interval of 45 minutes after 2 hours of smoking.

8. Also, add woodchips when the smoke decreases. Keep adding water and apple juice from time to time.

9. Once the pork is well smoked and reached the correct temperature, cut it into pieces and make a tent with the aluminum foil.

10. Let the meat rest for about 20 minutes and slice it evenly.

11. Your dish is ready to be served.

SMOKY ITALIAN SAUSAGES

SERVING SIZE: 1

SERVINGS PER RECIPE: 4

CALORIES: 234

COOKING TIME: 3 HOURS

INGREDIENTS:

Fresh Italian sausage—2 pounds

NUTRITION INFORMATION:

Carbohydrate—3 g

Protein—13 g

Fat—19 g

Sodium—831 mg

Cholesterol—39 mg

INSTRUCTIONS:
1. Set up the smoker at a temperature of 250°F.
2. You can cut the Italian sausages into halves or keep them as a whole.
3. Take out the electric smoker's rack and place the sausages on it. Maintain a gap of ½ inch between the Italian sausages to avoid sticking.
4. Let it smoke for about 3 hours or until the internal temperature reaches about 165°F.
5. Your dish is ready to be served.

PINEAPPLE AND HONEY GLAZED SMOKED HAM

SERVING SIZE: 1
SERVINGS PER RECIPE: 10
CALORIES: 434
COOKING TIME: 6 HOURS

INGREDIENTS:

- Ham—6 pounds, ready to eat
- Pineapple juice—1 cup
- Chicken stock—¾ cup
- Honey—½ cup
- Vegetable oil—2 tablespoons
- Black pepper—1 tablespoon
- Paprika—1 tablespoon
- Sugar—1 tablespoon
- Salt—2 teaspoons
- Dry mustard—2 teaspoons
- Cayenne—½ teaspoon
- Ground cloves—½ teaspoon

NUTRITION INFORMATION:

- Carbohydrate—20 g
- Protein—41 g
- Fat—21 g
- Sodium—334 mg
- Cholesterol—147 mg

INSTRUCTIONS:

1. In a bowl, add paprika, cayenne, and 1 teaspoon of dry mustard, sugar, salt, and pepper in it. Combine it together.

2. Take a plate and place the ham on it. Rub the prepared mixture all over the ham from all sides. Now cover the ham with a foil and let it refrigerate overnight.

3. Once the ham is taken out of the refrigerator, let it rest at room temperature for about an hour. Remove the foil from the ham.

4. Now set the electric smoker ready and adjust the temperature to 210°F. Place the ham on the smoker rack and let it smoke for about 6 hours.

5. Take another bowl and add chicken stock, ½ teaspoon of dry mustard, ¾ cup of pineapple juice, vegetable oil, and cloves in it. Mix them together. Let it heat over medium-high heat until everything is fully combined.

6. Now place the ham inside the smoker and keep drizzling the sauce all over it in every hour.

7. In a small bowl, add ¼ cup of pineapple juice, ½ teaspoon of dry mustard, honey, and ground cloves in it. Mix them together to prepare the glaze.

8. In the last hour of smoking, brush the glaze all over the pork. Keep repeating this step quite a number of times.

9. Once finished smoking, take it out from the smoker.

10. Your dish is ready to be served.

SMOKED PORK BELLY IN CHAR SIU SAUCE

SERVING SIZE: 1
SERVINGS PER RECIPE: 6
CALORIES: 531
COOKING TIME: 5 HOURS

INGREDIENTS:

Char siu sauce—½ cup

Pineapple juice—½ cup

Garlic cloves—5, finely minced

Kosher salt—1 tablespoon

Freshly ground black pepper—1 teaspoon

Pork belly—4 pounds, skin on

NUTRITION INFORMATION:

Carbohydrate—10 g

Protein—21 g

Fat—120 g

Sodium—1,130 mg

Cholesterol—165 mg

INSTRUCTIONS:

1. In a bowl, add char siu sauce, black pepper, garlic, pineapple juice, and salt. Mix them together.

2. Take a plate and put the pork belly in it. With the help of a knife, score the skin of the pork belly diagonally in every 2–3 inches. Repeat the same process in the opposite direction too. The entire pattern on the skin of the pork belly should look like a diamond shape.

3. In a ziplock bag, put the pork belly and pour the mix into it. Toss it well to ensure the pork belly is well coated in the marinade mix. Refrigerate it overnight.

4. Take out the pork belly from the refrigerator and set up the Masterbuilt ElectricSmoker at a temperature of 225°F.

5. Place the pork belly on the smoker rack with its skin side facing upward. Put it inside the smoker and allow it to smoke for nearly about 4 hours. Let it smoke until the internal temperature reads 160°F.

6. To make the skin of the pork belly crispy, put it inside the broiler on a medium-high heat. Once done, take it out from the broiler and allow it to cool down for about 15 minutes.

7. Place the pork belly on a plate and slice it evenly into pieces.

8. Your dish is ready to be served.

SMOKED HAWAIIAN KALUA PORK

SERVING SIZE: 1

SERVINGS PER RECIPE: 7

CALORIES: 269

COOKING TIME: 9 HOURS

INGREDIENTS:

Pork shoulder—4 pounds

Hawaiian pink sea salt—1 ½ teaspoons

Banana leaves

NUTRITION INFORMATION:

Carbohydrate—0 g

Protein—19 g

Fat—20 g

Sodium—59 mg

Cholesterol—79 mg

INSTRUCTIONS:
1. First of all, preheat the Masterbuilt Electric Smoker to a temperature of 200°F.

2. Place the pork on a plate and rub the Hawaiian sea salt all over the pork.

3. With the help of banana leaves, wrap the pork in it. To make it stay together, tie it with kitchen twine.

4. Put the wrapped pork inside the smoker rack and allow it to roast for about 8 hours at a temperature of 200°F. To make sure the meat is cooked thoroughly, let it cook until it reaches the internal temperature of 190°F.

5. Take out the meat from the smoker and let it rest for about 10 minutes.

6. Unwrap the banana leaves from the smoked pork meat and pair it up with steamed rice. Your dish is ready to be served.

BEEF RECIPES USING MASTERBUILT SMOKER

BON MOLASSES BEEF JERKY

SERVING SIZE: 1
SERVINGS PER RECIPE: 8
CALORIES: 252
COOKING TIME: 5 HOURS

INGREDIENTS:

- Beef roast—7 pounds
- Kentucky bourbon—1 cup
- Brown sugar—1/3 cup
- Pepper—2 teaspoons
- Soy sauce—1/3 cup
- Worcestershire—4 tablespoons
- Apple cider vinegar—4 tablespoons
- Molasses—4 tablespoons
- Red pepper flakes—½ teaspoon

NUTRITION INFORMATION:

- Carbohydrate—12g
- Protein—34g
- Fat—9 g
- Sodium—37 mg
- Cholesterol—12 mg

INSTRUCTIONS:

1. Take a large bowl and add all the ingredients in it. Mix it well.

2. Put the beef roast on a plate and slice it into ¼-inch thin strips. Get rid of the excess fat.

3. Put the beef strips in the marinade mix and cover it. Allow it to marinate in the refrigerator for about 16 hours or more.

4. Take out the beef strips from the marinade and pat it dry.

5. Set the temperature of the Masterbuilt Electric Smoker at 165°F.

6. Put apple woodchips at an interval of 1 hour each. Keep the top vent of the cooker half-open.

7. Place the beef strips on the rack and allow it to cook.

8. Take out the wood tray after an hour to let the air circulation to flow properly.

9. Let it cook until the beef begins to crack and bent. Let it cook for about 5 hours.

10. Your dish is ready to be served.

BEEF RUMP ROAST

SERVING SIZE: 1
SERVINGS PER RECIPE: 6
CALORIES: 195
COOKING TIME: 3 HOURS AND 30 MINUTES

INGREDIENTS:

- Beef rump roast—3 pounds
- Beef broth—2 cups
- Yellow mustard
- Texas rump rub

NUTRITION INFORMATION:

- Carbohydrate—2 g
- Protein—29 g
- Fat—7 g
- Sodium—55 mg
- Cholesterol—134 mg

INSTRUCTIONS:
1. Take a plate and place the rump roast on it.

2. Rub mustard on all sides of the rump roast. Season it with the Texas rump rub.

3. In a pan, pour the beef broth in it. Place the rump roast in the pan with its fat side facing upward.

4. Set up the smoker ready at a temperature of 225°F.

5. Put the uncovered pan along with the beef rump roast inside the electric smoker. Let it smoke for about 3 hours at a temperature of 135°F. Smoke it until the meat reaches the medium-rare doneness.

6. Beside the rump roast, add some vegetables on the pan inside the electric smoker such as carrots, onions, celery, and potatoes.

7. Once the internal temperature reaches 135°F, take out the meat from the smoker.

8. Now cover the rump roast with an aluminum foil and let it rest for about 10 minutes.

9. With the help of a knife, slice the beef roast into thin slices.

10. Your dish is ready to be served.

SMOKED CORNED BEEF

SERVING SIZE: 1

SERVINGS PER RECIPE: 10

CALORIES: 346

COOKING TIME: 7 HOURS

INGREDIENTS:

- Onion—1, medium, chopped
- Bacon—8 ounces, chopped
- Head of cabbage—1, roughly chopped
- Salt—to taste
- Pepper—to taste
- Corned beef—3–4
- Heavy-duty tin foil

NUTRITION INFORMATION:

- Carbohydrate—38 g
- Protein—18 g
- Fat—14 g
- Sodium—848 mg
- Cholesterol—68 mg

INSTRUCTIONS:

1. To prepare the cabbage, take a skillet and add chopped bacon in it first. Let the bacon cook until it turns brown in color.

2. Once the bacon is cooked, remove it from the pan and also reserve the bacon grease. Put chopped onions in it and sauté it until brown in color. Put in the roughly chopped cabbage and also toss the salad on medium-high heat with the help of two spoons. Toss the cabbage while it cooks. Put the prepared bacon in the skillet and toss them together.

3. Now to prepare the smoked corned beef, soak the corned beef in the water for about an hour. Take it out from the water and pat it dry with the help of a paper towel.

4. Sprinkle the seasoning packet on the corned beef and also on the top of the fat.

5. Set up the Masterbuilt ElectricSmoker and put the seasoned beef in it. Make sure the fat side of the beef is facing upward. Let it smoke at a temperature of 215°F for about 3 hours.

6. Once the smoking process is almost over, wrap the corned beef with a tinfoil. Add an ounce of water in the tinfoil. Make sure it is well wrapped from all sides. Allow it to smoke it for about 4 hours at a temperature of 215°F. Check whether the meat turns tender or not.

7. Once the beef is fully smoked, take it out from the electric smoker and slice the beef into thin strips.

8. Your dish is ready to be served.

SMOKED BEEF TRI-TIP ROAST

SERVING SIZE: 1
SERVINGS PER RECIPE: 6
CALORIES: 261
COOKING TIME: 2 HOURS

INGREDIENTS:

- Tri-tip roast—3 pounds
- Sea salt—2 teaspoons
- Mild chili powder—1 teaspoon
- Black pepper—1 teaspoon
- Brown sugar—1 teaspoon
- Espresso powder—1 teaspoon
- Onion powder—1 teaspoon
- Garlic powder—½ teaspoon
- Water
- Aluminum foil
- Cherry woodchips

NUTRITION INFORMATION:

- Carbohydrate—10 g
- Protein—37g
- Fat—16 g
- Sodium—271 mg
- Cholesterol—13 mg

INSTRUCTIONS:

1. Take a small bowl and add all the rub ingredients in it.

2. Place the tri-tip roast on a chopping board and with the help of a knife, score the meat diagonally. Make sure you keep 2-inch gap while scoring it. Repeat the process from the other direction to create a diamond pattern.

3. Season the roast with the rub mixture from all sides. Set the roast aside in the room temperature for about 30 minutes.

4. Put a bowl of water in the bottom of the electric smoker along with the woodchips in the side tray to create a good amount of smoke.

5. Preheat the electric smoker to a temperature of 225°F.

6. Put the tri-tip on the smoker rack with its fat side facing upward. Let it smoke for about 2 hours for a medium-rare doneness. Ideally, let it smoke for about 135°F.

7. Take out the roast from the electric smoker and tent it with a foil for about 20 minutes. This is done to allow the meat to absorb the juices.

8. Place the roast on the cutting board and slice it thinly.

9. Your dish is ready to be served.

SMOKED MEATLOAF

SERVING SIZE: 1
SERVINGS PER RECIPE: 5
CALORIES: 353
COOKING TIME: 4 HOURS

INGREDIENTS:

- Ground beef chuck—1 ¼ pounds
- Ground turkey—1 ¼ pounds
- Ground pork—1 pound
- Red bell peppers—1, roasted and chopped
- Fresh breadcrumbs—¾ cup
- Onion—1/3 cup, finely chopped
- Garlic cloves—4, fresh, minced
- Eggs—2, beaten
- Dried oregano—1 tablespoon
- Kosher salt—1 teaspoon
- Black pepper—½ teaspoon
- Barbeque sauce—1 ½ cups
- Aluminum foil

NUTRITION INFORMATION:

- Carbohydrate—14 g
- Protein—55 g
- Fat—39 g
- Sodium—565 mg
- Cholesterol—228 mg

INSTRUCTIONS:

1. To roast the red bell peppers, put it on a charcoal grill. Let it grill for about 15 minutes. Take off the blackened pepper skins and the seeds from it.

2. Do not rinse the grilled bell pepper. Place it on a chopping board and chop it well. Set it aside.

3. In a large bowl, add the ingredients and mix it well. Add ½ cup of the barbeque sauce in it. Keep the other half of the barbeque sauce for a later step. Mix all the ingredients together and combine it well.

4. In a pan, put a baking sheet on it. Mold the sides of the pan with an aluminum sheet with its side facing upward.

5. Pour the meatloaf mixture into it and set it aside.

6. Set up the smoker at a temperature of 225°F. Take the electric smoker rack and place the meatloaf pan on it. Put it inside the Masterbuilt ElectricSmoker and let it smoke for about 3 hours. Allow it to smoke until the beef reaches an internal temperature of 165°F.

7. Brush the reserved barbeque sauce all over the smoked meat and let it smoke for some more time.

8. Take out the smoked meatloaf from the electric smoker and allow it to cool down for about 2 minutes. Remove the pan and then cut the smoked meat into slices. Your dish is ready to be served.

SMOKED BEEF TENDERLOIN

SERVING SIZE: 3 OUNCES
SERVINGS PER RECIPE: 16
CALORIES: 226
COOKING TIME: 2 HOURS AND 20 MINUTES

INGREDIENTS:

Beef tenderloin—1, 4 pounds, trimmed, tied with kitchen twine

Kosher salt—4 teaspoons

Coarsely ground black pepper—3 teaspoons

NUTRITION INFORMATION:

Carbohydrate—0 g

Protein—35 g

Fat—9.5 g

Sodium—547 mg

Cholesterol—106 mg

INSTRUCTIONS:
1. Place the beef on a plate and season it well with salt and pepper. Refrigerate the beef for about 8 hours.

2. Set up the Masterbuilt ElectricSmoker according to the manufacturer's instructions. Take out the beef from the refrigerator and put it on the smoker rack. Allow it to smoke until the beef reaches an internal temperature of about 325°F. Let the beef smoke in this temperature for about 20 minutes.

3. To ensure the thicker portion of the beef is well smoked, cook the beef for about 50 minutes at a temperature of 125°F. In between this process, make sure to turn the beef over on the other side and smoke it well.

4. Now transfer the beef on a cutting board and allow it to rest for about 15 minutes. With the help of a knife, slice the beef into thin slices.

5. Your dish is ready to be served.

SMOKED BEEF JERKY

SERVING SIZE: 1
SERVINGS PER RECIPE: 6
CALORIES: 145
COOKING TIME: 6 HOURS

INGREDIENTS:

- Beef—1 pound
- Soy sauce—½ cup
- Worcestershire sauce—2 tablespoons
- Honey—2 tablespoons
- Red pepper flakes—1 tablespoon
- Onion powder—2 teaspoons
- Garlic powder—2 teaspoons
- Black pepper—1 teaspoon

NUTRITION INFORMATION:

- Carbohydrate—7 g
- Protein—11 g
- Fat—1 g
- Sodium—490 mg
- Cholesterol—30 mg